Ready Steady Maths

Teacher's Handbook

Carroll
Heinemann

Carroll Heinemann
Units 17-18
Willow Road Business Park
Knockmitten Lane
Dublin 12

Copyright © Mary Hurley and Ber O'Sullivan, 2000
Managing Editor: Gabrielle Jacob
Design: Susan Clarke

First published August 2000

ISBN 1 903574 02 1

Contents

Preface

'From the rectangles on the windows to the colours of the children's coats, the school environment is a Maths lesson waiting to happen.'
Mary Hurley and Ber O'Sullivan

Ready Steady Maths Stage One Teacher's Handbook is designed to complement and enhance *Ready Steady Maths* Stage One pupil's activity books. It contains ideas for activities that have the potential for rich and varied mathematical experience, as well as providing a user-friendly classroom tool specifically geared to the requirements of the *Primary School Curriculum* (1999).

The exercises in the pupil's books allow children to demonstrate their understanding of concepts introduced, developed and evaluated in class. These exercises have been deliberately pared down to ensure that the recording of Maths is fun, interesting and well within the capabilities of all children.

The aim of the programme as a whole is to promote the following skills:
- communicating and exploring mathematical concepts
- applying and problem-solving
- integrating and connecting
- reasoning
- estimating, predicting and recording
- understanding and recalling

How the book is organised

Ready Steady Maths Stage One Teacher's Handbook consists of five sections:
- Introduction (strategies/methodologies/assessment/materials)
- Junior Infants
- Senior Infants
- Additional activities
- Curriculum planners

The 'Introduction' outlines the uses of the book as well as detailing strategies and methodologies for the classroom.

Both the Junior and Senior Infant sections are comprised of detailed explorations of each of the Strands of the *Primary School Curriculum*, a bank of photocopiable masters and an assessment grid. Each Strand module is presented as shown below.

The section 'Additional Activities' provides a bank of further activities including:
- uses of the number line
- ideas for counting on and counting back
- uses of the 'magic box'
- ideas for planning a Maths trail

The 'Curriculum Planner' section consists of full-colour page-by-page outlines of each of the three pupil's activity books.

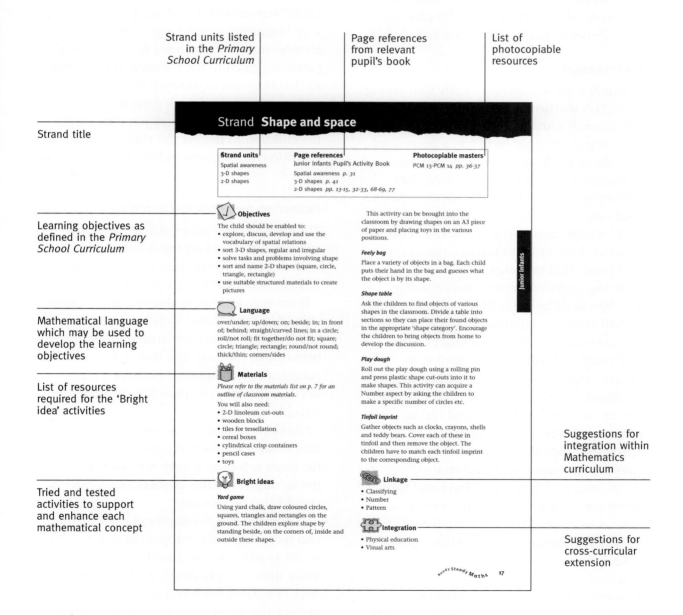

Strand units listed in the *Primary School Curriculum*

Page references from relevant pupil's book

List of photocopiable resources

Strand title

Learning objectives as defined in the *Primary School Curriculum*

Mathematical language which may be used to develop the learning objectives

List of resources required for the 'Bright idea' activities

Tried and tested activities to support and enhance each mathematical concept

Suggestions for integration within Mathematics curriculum

Suggestions for cross-curricular extension

Strand **Shape and space**

Strand units
Spatial awareness
3-D shapes
2-D shapes

Page references
Junior Infants Pupil's Activity Book
Spatial awareness *p. 31*
3-D shapes *p. 41*
2-D shapes *pp. 13-15, 32-33, 68-69, 77*

Photocopiable masters
PCM 13-PCM 14 *pp. 36-37*

Objectives
The child should be enabled to:
- explore, discuss, develop and use the vocabulary of spatial relations
- sort 3-D shapes, regular and irregular
- solve tasks and problems involving shape
- sort and name 2-D shapes (square, circle, triangle, rectangle)
- use suitable structured materials to create pictures

Language
over/under; up/down; on; beside; in; in front of; behind; straight/curved lines; in a circle; roll/not roll; fit together/do not fit; square; circle; triangle; rectangle; round/not round; thick/thin; corners/sides

Materials
Please refer to the materials list on p. 7 for an outline of classroom materials.
You will also need:
- 2-D linoleum cut-outs
- wooden blocks
- tiles for tessellation
- cereal boxes
- cylindrical crisp containers
- pencil cases
- toys

Bright ideas

Yard game
Using yard chalk, draw coloured circles, squares, triangles and rectangles on the ground. The children explore shape by standing beside, on the corners of, inside and outside these shapes.

This activity can be brought into the classroom by drawing shapes on an A3 piece of paper and placing toys in the various positions.

Feely bag
Place a variety of objects in a bag. Each child puts their hand in the bag and guesses what the object is by its shape.

Shape table
Ask the children to find objects of various shapes in the classroom. Divide a table into sections so they can place their found objects in the appropriate 'shape category'. Encourage the children to bring objects from home to develop the discussion.

Play dough
Roll out the play dough using a rolling pin and press plastic shape cut-outs into it to make shapes. This activity can acquire a Number aspect by asking the children to make a specific number of circles etc.

Tinfoil imprint
Gather objects such as clocks, crayons, shells and teddy bears. Cover each of these in tinfoil and then remove the object. The children have to match each tinfoil imprint to the corresponding object.

Linkage
- Classifying
- Number
- Pattern

Integration
- Physical education
- Visual arts

Junior Infants

Ready Steady Maths 17

Strategies and methodologies

Constructivism

The constructivist approach is one recommended by the *Primary School Curriculum*. This approach holds that students construct understanding actively rather than absorbing information passively through didactic instruction. It is, therefore, vital that opportunities should be created for development of mathematical concepts through problem-solving situations, hands-on experience and social interaction.

By engaging in such activities, children are enabled to make sense of their experience and to develop understanding by creating 'links between new and existing knowledge'.

Oral language

Research indicates unequivocally that young children's mathematical attainment is significantly enhanced when they are regularly encouraged to talk in a purposeful way about the Maths in which they are engaging. The *Primary School Curriculum* emphasises that classroom discussion plays a vital role at every stage of Maths development and that this discussion can be child to child, child to teacher, teacher to child and child to group.

For the approach to work successfully, children must be trained in discussion skills, as well as in the dynamics of working with a partner or as a member of a small group. Skills such as taking turns, listening to others, responding positively to the opinions of others, clarity of expression; all of these can be nurtured in the safe and caring environment of the classroom.

In response to the *Primary School Curriculum*, a series of Strand-related, interactive, oral language 'Think and Talk' pages are included in the pupil's books at regular intervals. They are designed to:
- encourage discussion in class and group work
- extend vocabulary
- provide opportunities for revisiting concepts both to reinforce and to provide extension activities

Details are provided in the Junior and Senior Infant sections of this handbook.

Problem-solving

Children's attempts to solve a problem require them to call on many skills. Problem-solving experiences should therefore develop the ability to plan, take risks, learn from trial and error, check and evaluate solutions, and think logically.

Discussion and the acceptance of the points of view of others are also central to the development of problem-solving strategies. Building up the children's confidence in going with their instincts is vital. They should be encouraged from the very beginning to have a go and take a chance; however care must be taken that the problems given to the children are structured so that they can experience success.

The evaluation of work done through either group or class discussion encourages the children to respect the ideas of others, to try different solutions and to offer alternative ones.

Estimation, prediction and recording

Throughout the *Primary School Curriculum*, emphasis is placed on the development of estimation and prediction strategies. These skills are essential for real life Maths.

From very early in Junior Infants, children should be encouraged to estimate. Young children find it very difficult to differentiate between an estimate and the answer. So constant encouragement to 'have a guess' is needed, though it is important to elicit a sensible guess.

Children should be encouraged to realise that while estimation is a help towards finding a solution, it may not necessarily be the solution. The fun element of estimation should also be stressed.

To assist in the development of estimation and recording skills, puppet characters such as 'Mr Guess' and Mrs Count' can be used. To make these, simply attach a lollipop to the back of a paper plate and draw a face on the front. Using these, any activity can acquire an estimation and recording aspect.

Recording itself may be performed in a variety of ways including written, concrete, oral and pictorial. Photographs can be used as a permanent record of work done in class, as well as providing wonderful topics for discussion and revisiting.

Revisiting

The importance of revisiting work already covered cannot be overestimated. Children enjoy returning to concepts already mastered and it reinforces the work while allowing the children to shine. It also offers opportunities for greater development of the concept, as well as allowing the children to explore other methods of performing the activity.

Assessment

Assessment is an integral part of the teaching and learning process. Teachers use assessment techniques every day. They make decisions about what to teach and how to teach it, based on their observation and the feedback they receive from work the children are doing.

To assist in the assessment process and in line with the emphasis of the *Primary School Curriculum* that 'assessment should look at the whole child and consider both the processes of the child's learning and the product of that learning', Junior and Senior Infant assessment grids are provided. These grids are based on teacher observation and teacher-designed class tasks, as well as the day-to-day work of the class.

It is intended that the grids should be photocopied from the handbook and assembled or added to the teacher's file. Each element of each Strand Unit is detailed and only requires a simple mark to show that the concept has been understood and acquired.

Materials

Bought

- Pegs and pegboards
- Counters (dinosaurs, bears, frogs etc.)
- Sorting trays
- Multilink cubes
- 2-D and 3-D shapes
- Octagons
- Construction straws
- Balances
- Egg timers (30 second; 1 minute; 2 minute)
- Clocks and clock stamps
- Scissors
- Plasticine
- Mobilo
- Linkets
- Gears
- Beads
- Lego
- Large dice
- Money and money stamps
- Large clothes pegs
- Yard chalk
- Coloured plastic cellophane
- Elastic bands
- 2cm^2 stamps

Found

- Spools
- Shells
- Stones
- Conkers and cones
- Topical small toys
- Plastic juice bottles
- Yoghurt cartons
- Cylindrical crisp containers
- Shoe boxes
- Old magazines
- Bottle tops
- Corks
- Linoleum
- Carpet samples

Pupil's name	Counting	Comparing & ordering		
	Count objects 1-20	Compare equivalent and non-equivalent sets 0-10	Order sets by number 0-10	Language of ordinal number

In order to explore the full potential of all the equipment listed, it is important that the children be allowed to play freely with the materials. It is only through play and the infusion of their imagination into the work that children discover the innumerable possibilities of the equipment. In fact, the children's shared experience is one of the most useful teaching tools available to the teacher!

Junior Infants

September Starter

Page 23: Teddy bears' picnic

Early mathematical activities: Comparing
Early mathematical activities: Classifying
Number: Counting
Algebra: Extending patterns
Shape and space: Spatial awareness
Measures: Time

Page 24: In the adventure playground

Early mathematical activities: Comparing
Early mathematical activities: Classifying
Number: Counting
Shape and space: Spatial awareness

Junior Infants Activity Book

Page 7: Jack and the beanstalk

Early mathematical activities: Comparing
Early mathematical activities: Ordering
Number: Counting
Measures: Length

Page 10: Size

Early mathematical activities: Comparing
Algebra: Extending patterns
Measures: Length

Page 31: The pond

Number: Comparing and ordering
Number: Counting
Number: Analysis of number
Shape and space: Spatial awareness

Page 41: Shapes

Number: Counting
Number: Comparing and ordering

Shape and space: 3-D shapes

Page 45: Heavy and light

Measures: Weight

Page 52: Time

Measures: Time

Page 66: Narrow and wide

Measures: Length

Page 73: Empty set

Number: Numeration

Page 79: Data

Data: Recognising and interpreting data

Page 80: Data

Number: Counting
Shape and space: 2-D shapes
Data: recognising and interpreting data

Page 85: Townscape

Number: Counting
Algebra: Extending patterns
Measures: Time

Page 90: Countdown

Number: Counting
Number: Numeration

Page 94: Bug trail

Number: Counting
Data: Recognising and interpreting data

Problem-solving

Photocopiable master

PCM 1 *p. 24*

While no formal problem-solving pages are included in the Junior Infant pupil's books, problem-solving techniques can be introduced during the year. Some of the oral language pages may be used for this purpose (see below).

Children should work collaboratively, either in pairs or small groups as this assists in the development of communicative skills. The use of manipulatives and concrete materials also assists in this process as the children describe what they observe and what they do with the counters etc.

Page 31: The pond

Begin by exploring the language potential of the page.

Using carpet squares as lilypads and frog counters or cubes, illustrate a story about the page.

Divide the class into pairs and encourage the children to develop and enact stories; one child may tell a story while the other enacts it using the counters. The activity may be recorded pictorially or using Plasticine.

The teacher sits with each group in turn encouraging discussion. When each pair has had the opportunity to tease out their response, there is feedback to the class.

The activity may be extended into the playground by drawing lilypads using yard chalk and encouraging the children to enact their stories by moving from one lilypad to the next.

Junior Infants

Strand units	Page references	Photocopiable master
Classifying	Junior Infants September Starter	PCM 2 *p. 25*
Matching	Classifying *pp. 2-15, 18-19*	
Comparing	Matching *pp. 16-17, 20-22*	
Ordering	Comparing *pp. 23-24*	

Page references

Junior Infants Pupil's Activity Book

Classifying *pp. 1-2, 4*
Matching *pp. 5-6, 11-12*
Comparing *pp. 3, 7-9*
Ordering *p. 10*

 Objectives

The child should be enabled to:
- classify objects on the basis of one attribute, such as colour, shape, texture or size
- identify the complement of a set (i.e. elements not in a set)
- match equivalent and non-equivalent sets using one-to-one correspondence
- compare objects according to length, width, height, quantity, thickness or size
- compare sets without counting
- order objects according to length or height
  - order sets without counting

 Language

more than/less than; as many as; long/short; longer/shorter; bigger/smaller; the same as; not the same; the same colour as; goes with; belongs to; each; enough/not enough

 Materials

Please refer to the materials list on p. 7 for an outline of classroom materials.

You will also need:
- lollipop sticks
- cuddly toys
- matching cards
- coloured bean-bags
- hula-hoops
- play food

 Bright ideas

Colour search

Ask the class to find all the items of a selected colour in the classroom. Using these, make a colour table. Encourage the children to bring in items from home to add to the table and develop the discussion of shades and tones.

Carpet islands

Place a number of carpet samples on the floor and scatter a variety of toys around them. Assign each 'island' to a different toy by placing a drawing of the designated item in the centre of each. The children have to sort the toys to their respective 'island.'

Hula-hoop sort

Place two hula-hoops on the ground and scatter coloured bean-bags around them. The children place all the bean-bags of a selected colour into one of the hoops and all the other bean-bags into the other hoop. This activity can be done in groups or by the entire class and could be performed in the playground, PE hall or classroom.

Find your coat

This is a simple activity that can be performed just before going home. Mix up the children's coats and ask them to find their own. This activity stimulates and encourages visual awareness.

Junior Infants

Sort it out

Put a mixture of counters into a number of shoe boxes. Divide the class into groups and give each group a box. Children sort the items in the box according to type and/or colour.

Matching

Use counters such as dinosaurs, bears and frogs to explore the concept of matching using defined attributes.

Teddy bears' picnic

Place a cloth on the floor and arrange a number of teddy bears in a circle on it. Each child is given responsibility for one bear and has to make sure that the bear has a mug, a plate and a piece of play food pizza. This activity can be performed in groups.

Put teddy to bed

Dress six shoe boxes as beds and place a teddy bear in each. The children explore the concepts of enough/sufficiency by removing both beds and teddy bears in varying numbers.

Lots of lollies

Give each child some lollipop sticks and plastic bottle tops or a ball of Plasticine. The children use the materials to make as many lollipops as they can. The discussion focuses on the language of sufficiency.

Kim's game

Place a number of toys (not more than five) on the table. Encourage the children to look at and discuss them. Cover the table with a cloth and remove one of the toys. Uncover the table and ask the children to tell you which toy is missing. This game can be played regularly and the difficulty level increased by removing more objects.

 **Linkage**

- Number
- Shape
- Colour

 **Integration**

- Visual arts

Strand units	Page references	Photocopiable masters
Counting	Junior Infants Pupil's Activity Book	PCM 3-PCM 12 *pp. 26-35*
Comparing and ordering	Comparing and ordering *pp. 55, 57, 89, 92*	
Analysis of number	One / 1 *pp. 16-19*	
• Combining	Two / 2 *pp. 24-29*	
• Partitioning	Revisit 1–2 *p. 30*	
• Numeration	Three / 3 *pp. 34-39*	
	Revisit 1–3 *p. 40*	
	Four / 4 *pp. 46-50*	
	Revisit 1–4 *pp. 51, 53-54*	
	Five / 5 *pp. 58-63*	
	Revisit 1–5 *pp. 64-65, 71-72, 75, 84, 90-91, 93*	
	Zero / 0 *pp. 73-74*	
	Combining *pp. 81-83*	

 Objectives

The child should be enabled to:
- count the objects in a set (1-10)
- compare equivalent and non-equivalent sets (1-5) by matching without using symbols
- order sets of objects by number (1-5)
- use the language of ordinal number (first; last)
- explore the components of number (1-5)
- combine sets of objects, totals to 5
- partition sets of objects (1-5)
- develop an understanding of the conservation of number (1-5)
- read, write and order numerals (1-5)
- identify the empty set and the numeral zero
- subitise the number of objects in a set (1-5)
- solve simple oral problems (0-5)

 Language

more than/less than; the same as; how many?; copy; count; first/last; and; make

 Materials

Please refer to the materials list on p. 7 for an outline of classroom materials.

You will also need:
- stickers
- broad beans
- gold spray

 **Bright ideas
(counting and combining)**

Pinned on me

Place a sticker with a numeral (1-5) on it on one child's back. The rest of the children have to give the child clues as to the number without actually saying what it is.

Finger count up

The class counts in unison up to 10, holding up one finger for each number counted until all ten fingers are up. They then count back down to zero, putting their fingers down as they go. This activity takes practice as finger co-ordination is difficult.

Target circle

Seat the children in a circle. Choose a target number and ask the children to count to ten. The child who says the target number stands.

Number clap

Seat the children in a circle and start a number clap. When the circle has completed, change the clap and go around the circle again. As the children grow accustomed to this, rhythm patterns emerge.

Number trains

Choose five children and give each of them a placard with a number (1-5) written on it. These children are the train drivers. Divide the rest of the children into groups of passengers waiting for the train. Blow a whistle and the trains move off to music. Each train stops at each group and picks up one passenger. The activity continues until the number on each placard is reached.

Number islands

Place a number of carpet samples on the floor and scatter a range of toys around them. On each one, place a number label. The children have to place the appropriate number of toys on each 'island'.

Family islands

Place two carpet samples on the floor. On one, place two cardboard cut-out figures. On the other, place three. The children have to find different ways of combining the families and talk about it.

Broad beans count

Spray a large number of broad beans with gold spray on one side. Give each child a number of beans. The children shuffle the beans, throw them on the table and discuss the results. This activity assists in the development of prediction skills.

Hula-hoop count

In the PE hall, the children throw beanbags into hula-hoops. The discussion focuses on the numbers that land inside and outside the hoops.

Number books 1- 5

Children either draw or cut out pictures to make their books of one, two, three, four and five. These books can be used for reinforcement and revisiting.

 **Linkage**

- Colour
- Shape
- Size
- Length
- Height

 Integration

- Visual arts
- Physical education
- Music
- Language

Strand **Algebra**

Strand unit	**Page references**
Extending patterns	Junior Infants Pupil's Activity Book
	Extending patterns *pp. 42-44, 85, 87*

 Objectives

The child should be enabled to:
• identify, copy and extend patterns in colour, shape and size

 Language

pattern; shape; colour; size; copy; what comes next?; design your own pattern

 Materials

Please refer to the materials list on p. 7 for an outline of classroom materials.

You will also need:
• children's toys

 Bright ideas

Lunch patterns

Use the children's lunches to lay out the food and beverages in different patterns, such as drink I food I drink I food.

Beat it out

Seat the children in a circle or stand them in a line and begin a clap pattern. The children continue the sound pattern. This activity requires practice but the patterns can become more complex as the children become acquainted with the dynamic.

Body patterns

Seat the children in a line and encourage them to experiment with body patterns, such as sit I stand I sit I stand.

Lining up

Simple patterns can be done while waiting to go out or come in, such as hands up I hands down or hands in I hands out.

Plan your pattern

Encourage the children to explore pattern by making necklaces of coloured beads and multicoloured towers of multilink cubes. Each child is given a task using beads or cubes e.g. red and yellow. The children then make as many patterns as they can using the manipulatives. Discussion focuses on the language of pattern and children should actively talk about the patterns they have created using manipulatives.

 **Linkage**

• Number
• Shape
• Colour
• Size
• Counting

 Integration

• Visual arts
• Geography

Strand units	Page references	Photocopiable masters
Spatial awareness	Junior Infants Pupil's Activity Book	PCM 13-PCM 14 *pp. 36-37*
3-D shapes	Spatial awareness *p. 31*	
2-D shapes	3-D shapes *p. 41*	
	2-D shapes *pp. 13-15, 32-33, 68-69, 77, 86*	

Objectives

The child should be enabled to:
- explore, discuss, develop and use the vocabulary of spatial relations
- sort 3-D shapes, regular and irregular
- solve tasks and problems involving shape
- sort and name 2-D shapes (square, circle, triangle, rectangle)
- use suitable structured materials to create pictures

Language

over/under; up/down; on; beside; in; in front of; behind; straight/curved lines; in a circle; roll/not roll; fit together/do not fit; square; circle; triangle; rectangle; round/not round; thick/thin; corners/sides

Materials

Please refer to the materials list on p. 7 for an outline of classroom materials.

You will also need:
- 2-D linoleum cut-outs
- wooden blocks
- tiles for tessellation
- cereal boxes
- cylindrical crisp containers
- pencil cases
- toys

Bright ideas

Yard game

Using yard chalk, draw coloured circles, squares, triangles and rectangles on the ground. The children explore shape by standing beside, on the corners of, inside and outside these shapes.

This activity can be brought into the classroom by drawing shapes on an A3 piece of paper and placing toys in the various positions.

Feely bag

Place a variety of objects in a bag. Each child puts their hand in the bag and guesses what the object is by its shape.

Shape table

Ask the children to find objects of various shapes in the classroom. Divide a table into sections so they can place their found objects in the appropriate 'shape category'. Encourage the children to bring objects from home to develop the discussion.

Play dough

Roll out the play dough using a rolling pin and press plastic shape cut-outs into it to make shapes. This activity can acquire a Number aspect by asking the children to make a specific number of circles etc.

Tinfoil imprint

Gather objects such as clocks, crayons, shells and teddy bears. Cover each of these in tinfoil and then remove the object. The children have to match each tinfoil imprint to the corresponding object.

Linkage

- Classifying
- Number
- Pattern

Integration

- Physical education
- Visual arts

Junior Infants

Strand unit	Page references
Length	Junior Infants Pupil's Activity Book
	Length *pp. 20-23, 66*

 Objectives

The child should be enabled to:
- develop an understanding of the concept of length through exploration, discussion and use of appropriate vocabulary
- compare and order objects according to length or height

 Language

long/short; tall/short; wide/narrow; longer/ shorter; wider than/narrower than; shorter than; the same length as

 Materials

Please refer to the materials list on p. 7 for an outline of classroom materials.

You will also need:
- ribbon
- friction cars
- newspaper
- peel-off dots
- empty plastic bottles
- cuddly toys

 Bright ideas

Walter Worm

Using Plasticine make Walter. Roll out two other pieces of Plasticine, one longer, one shorter, to complete the family.

Car race

Using yard chalk, mark a start line on the ground. Line up as many friction cars as required at the line and let them go. This activity allows the children to compare the distances travelled by the cars; these can be measured using a length of ribbon.

How tall

Pin a large sheet of newspaper to the wall. Each child stretches up to see how high he/she can reach. Mark each point with a peel-off dot and initial it so that during the year the height chart can be revisited and the children can see how much they have grown.

Sand trails

Take a number of differently-shaped empty plastic bottles and score a hole in the bottom of each. Fill each bottle with an equal quantity of sand. Each child takes two bottles and explores how far he/she can walk before the sand runs out. Encourage the children to walk in straight and meandering lines. This activity can be recorded pictorially.

Teddy bears' bed-time

Dress three shoe boxes as beds and select a teddy bear that fits in each. The children then explore length by deciding which bear belongs in which bed.

 Linkage

- Time
- Measures
- Number

 **Integration**

- Physical education
- Visual arts
- Language

Strand unit

Weight

Page reference

Junior Infants Pupil's Activity Book

Weight *p. 45*

 Objectives

The child should be enabled to:
- develop an understanding of the concept of weight through exploration, handling of objects and use of appropriate vocabulary
- compare objects according to weight

 Language

heavy/light; heavier/lighter; balance; weigh

 Materials

Please refer to the materials list on p. 7 for an outline of classroom materials.

You will also need:
- pencils
- bean-bags
- fruit and vegetables
- empty two litre and one litre plastic containers
- cuddly toys

 Bright ideas

Magic box

Place a number of objects including bottle corks, bean-bags, pencils and fruit in a box. The children close their eyes, put their hands in the box, select an object and guess what it might be by its weight. To extend this activity, each child selects two objects and compares their weights.

Fruit and vegetable stall

Set up a fruit and vegetable stall in the classroom, using a variety of fruit and vegetables. The children use the stall to explore the concept of weight by comparing different items.

Milk weigh

Fill a variety of plastic containers with water. Each child takes two different containers and places each one in a plastic carrier bag. By holding one bag in each hand, the children can explore the concept of comparative weight. This activity can be extended by filling the containers to different levels or not at all.

Which is heavier?

Using materials from the classroom, balance and compare the weights of different objects on the classroom kitchen scales.

Weigh a bear

The children weigh a collection of bears or cuddly toys using kitchen scales. Each toy can be weighed against multilink cubes or against other toys.

 Linkage

- Measures
- Number

Integration

- Geography
- Science
- Language

Strand unit	Page reference
Capacity	Junior Infants Pupil's Activity Book
	Capacity *p. 56*

Objectives

The child should be enabled to:
- develop an understanding of the concept of capacity through exploration and use of appropriate vocabulary
- compare containers according to capacity

Language

full/nearly full/empty; holds more/holds less/holds as much as

Materials

Please refer to the materials list on p. 7 for an outline of classroom materials.

You will also need:
- rice
- pasta
- marbles
- funnels
- sieves
- measuring spoons
- shoe boxes
- soft toys

Bright ideas

Fill it up

Encourage the children to explore the concept of capacity by filling various containers with water, sand, pasta or rice. They then pour out contents until empty. Alternatively, they can fill one container from another of a different size. This activity is used to encourage children to acquire and engage in the language of capacity.

Teddies at home

Number four shoe boxes one to four and place different numbers of teddy bears in each. The discussion centres on what houses are full, empty, half-full etc.

Milkman game

Using a variety of (washed) empty milk containers, encourage the children to play the role of milkman and experiment by filling and carrying them.

Sand game

Using a variety of implements and vessels, the children scoop sand into different containers. Discussion focuses on the different quantities required.

Talk about it

Divide the class into groups and give each group a set of containers with an elastic band around each one, to show the level to which it should be filled. The children fill each container as indicated while utilising the language of capacity.

Linkage
- Number
- Data
- Time

Integration
- Science

Strand **Measures (time)**

Strand unit	Page reference	Photocopiable masters
Time	Junior Infants Pupil's Activity Book	PCM 15-PCM 17 *pp. 38-40*
	Time *p. 52*	

Objectives

The child should be enabled to:
- develop an understanding of the concept of time through the use of appropriate vocabulary
- sequence daily events or stages in a story

Language

morning/evening; night/day; early/late; days of the week; lunchtime; bedtime; school days; weekend

Materials

Please refer to the materials list on p. 7 for an outline of classroom materials.

You will also need:
- clockwork toys
- large sheets of coloured paper

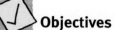

Bright ideas

Tidy up time

Challenge the class to see how long it takes to put things away and tidy the classroom. Alternatively, using a clockwork toy, ask the class how many things they think they can tidy away before the toy stops. This is an ideal opportunity to develop their predictive skills.

Shape hunt

Using an egg-timer, challenge the class to find as many objects of a designated shape or colour in the classroom before the sand runs out. This activity can be used for phonics work by asking the class to find objects beginning with a designated letter.

What time is it Mr Wolf?

This activity can be performed in the PE hall or playground. Taking the role of 'Mr Wolf', stand at one end of the hall or yard with your back to the children. The children chant, in unison, 'What time is it, Mr Wolf?' Answer with different times, for example, 'It's one o'clock!' The children take the appropriate number of steps for every hour that Mr Wolf says that it is. Eventually, announce that it's 'Dinner time', turn around and advance towards the children. The children rush to their 'den' before they are caught.

Time books

Divide a sheet of A2 paper vertically in two. Write 'Morning' and 'Afternoon' at the top of each column respectively. Discuss with the children what they do during the day and ask them to record their suggestions pictorially. Each picture is then pasted into the appropriate column.

Day and night frieze

Divide a sheet of A2 paper vertically in two. Write 'Day' and 'Night' at the top of each column respectively. Discuss with the children the differences between day and night and ask them to record their ideas pictorially. Each picture is then pasted into the appropriate area of the frieze.

Linkage

- Number
- Colour

Integration

- Visual arts
- Language

Junior Infants

Strand unit	Page references	Photocopiable master
Money	Junior Infants Pupil's Activity Book	PCM 18-PCM 19 *pp. 41-42*
	Money *pp. 67, 78*	(PCM 19 to be used from January 2002)

Objectives

The child should be enabled to:
- recognise and use coins (up to 5p/5 cents)
- solve practical tasks and problems using money

Language

buy; sell; spend; coins; pence/cents; how much?

Materials

Please refer to the materials list on p. 7 for an outline of classroom materials.

You will also need:
- an assortment of shops
- real coinage
- a toy cash register
- cornflakes
- egg cartons
- cuddly toys

Bright ideas

Class shop

Set up a play shop and alternate its wares regularly. This allows children to explore the concepts of buying and selling in a variety of shop environments.

Under my hand

Fill a box with a mixture of 1p/1 cent, 2p/2 cent and 5p/5 cent coins. Take a coin and hide it under your hand. Encourage the children to guess what the coin might be by examining the other coins in the box.

Cornflake count

Line up two rows of cornflakes. Each child chooses a line and takes it in turns to throw three coins together. If there are two heads, the child throwing eats two cornflakes from his/her line. If there are two tails, the child eats two cornflakes from the other team's line. The team whose cornflake line gets eaten first wins.

Egg carton count

Write different amounts on the cups of an egg carton. The children then place the appropriate amount of money in each cup.

Teddies go shopping

Line up a row of teddy bears and place a sticker bearing an amount on the front of each. The children place the appropriate number of coins in front of each bear.

Linkage
- Number

Integration
- Language
- Geography

Strand **Data**

Strand unit	Page references	Photocopiable master
Recognising and interpreting data	Junior Infants Pupil's Activity Book Recognising and interpreting data *pp. 70, 76, 79-80, 88, 94*	PCM 20 *p. 43*

Junior Infants

 Objectives

The child should be enabled to:
- sort and classify sets of objects by one criterion
- match sets, equal and unequal
- represent and interpret a set of simple mathematical data using real objects, models and pictures

 Language

more/less; more than/less than; as many as; the same as; enough; as much as

 Materials

Please refer to the materials list on p. 7 for an outline of classroom materials.

You will also need:
- hula-hoops
- marbles
- balls
- tin cans
- toy cars
- soft toys
- plastic toys

 Bright ideas

Carpet islands

Place a number of carpet samples on the floor and scatter a range of toys around them. There should be no more than five of any item. The children sort the toys by type, size or colour using the islands as sorting trays.

Hula-hoop game

Place two hula-hoops on the floor and scatter a range of objects around them including boxes, drink cartons, marbles, balls and cans. The children have to sort the items into those that roll and those that don't.

Car parks

The children match spaces to cars and compare the numbers of cars in different car parks. A 'spaces empty' board on the car park indicates the number of spaces left, and children can change this as each car enters or leaves.

Birthday hat

Using strips of cardboard, make three headbands. Affix the numerals 4, 5, and 6 to them respectively. Ask each child to make and decorate their own birthday hat, incorporating their age into the design. The class is then sorted by age into its respective groups, using the headbands as a focus.

Drinks

Collect empty drinks cartons from the children and use them to create a block graph of what the children drink. Use a metre stick as the base-line for the chart.

 **Linkage**

- Number
- Shape
- Colour
- Comparing and ordering

**Integration**

- Visual arts

I made
a great leap
today.

| 1 | 2 | 3 | 4 | 5 |

Write

| 1 | 2 | 3 | 4 | 5 |

Write

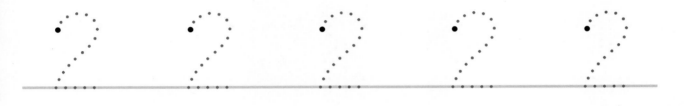

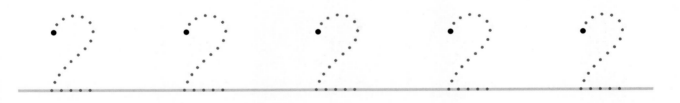

| 1 | 2 | 3 | 4 | 5 |

Write

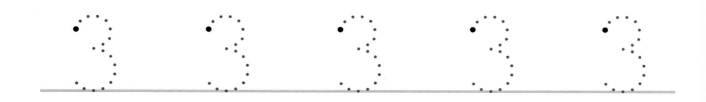

1	2	3	4	5

Write

1	2	3	4	5

Write

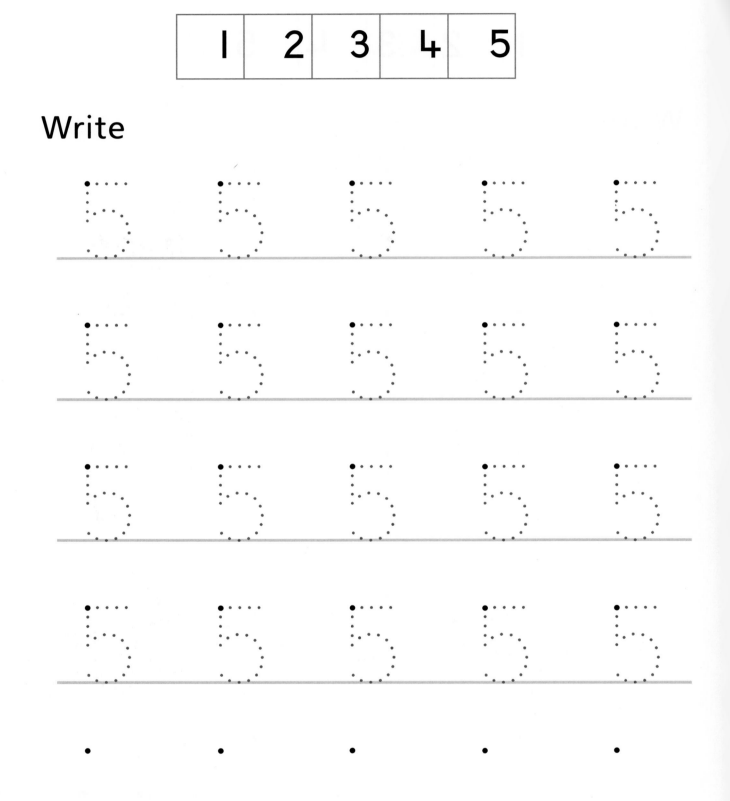

How many?

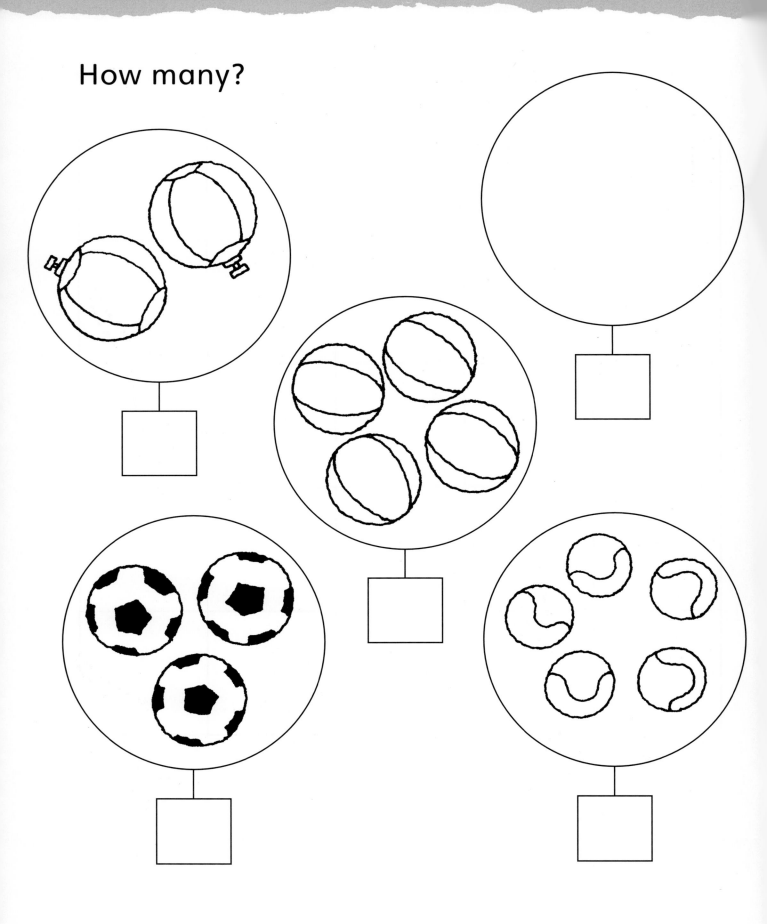

Draw the spots

Colour

Colour the things inside
Ring the things outside

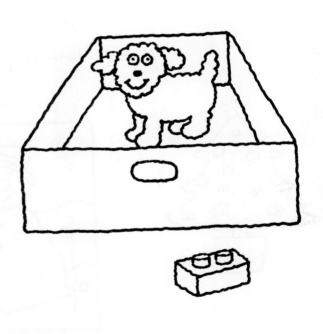

Colour

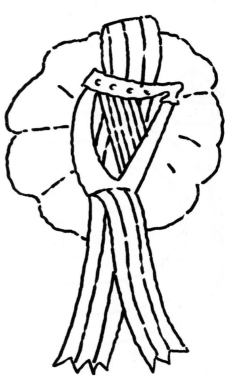

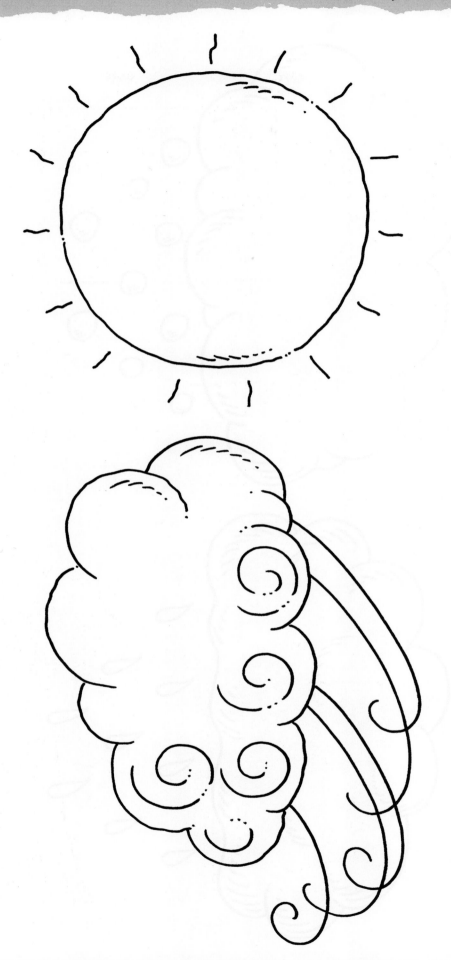

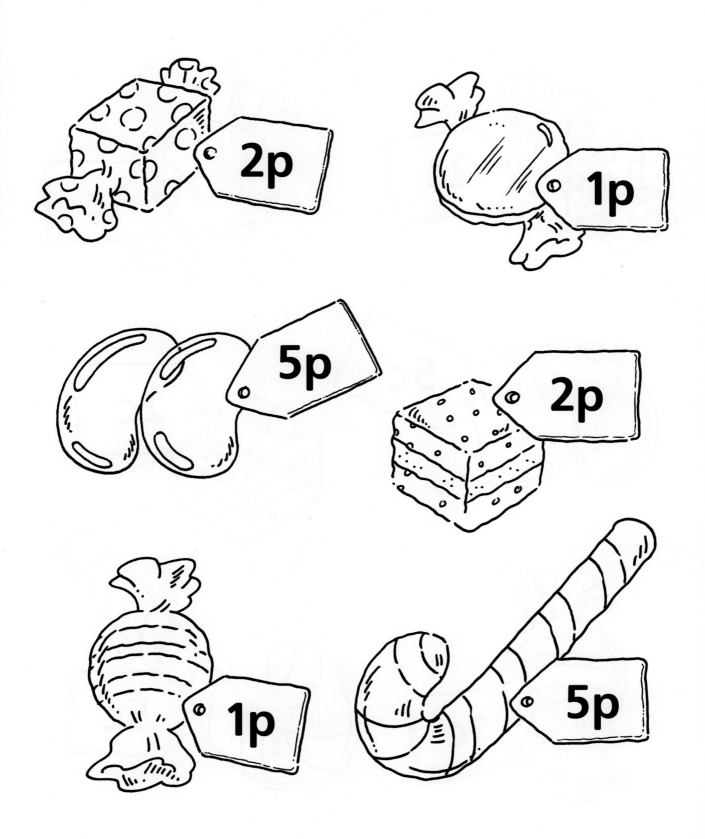

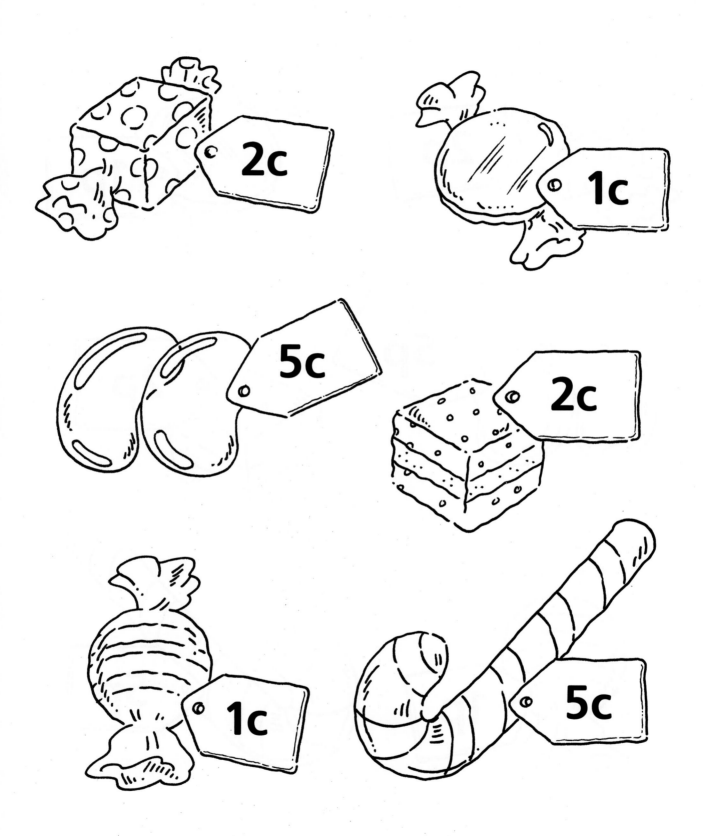

Guess

Count

Junior Infants

Pupil's name	Classifying					Matching				Comparing								
	Colour	Shape	Texture	Size	Elements not in a set	One-to-one correspondence	Related matching	Match equivalent sets	Match non-equivalent sets	Length	Width	Height	Weight	Quantity	Compare sets	Size	More than	Less than

Ordering			Counting	Comparing & ordering			Analysis of number								
Order by length	Order by height	Order sets without counting	Count objects 1-10	Compare and order equivalent and non-equivalent sets 1-5	Order sets by number 1-5	Language of ordinal number	Explore components of number 1-5	Combine sets of objects (totals to 5)	Partition sets of objects 1-5	Read numerals 1-5	Write numerals 1-5	Order numerals 1-5	Identify empty set	Identify numeral zero	Subitise sets	Solve oral problems

Algebra			Spatial awareness	3-D shapes		2-D shapes		Length			Weight		Capacity	Time		Money	Data
Copy and extend colour	Copy and extend shape	Copy and extend size	Language of spatial relations	Sort 3-D shapes	Perform shape tasks	Sort 2-D shapes	Perform shape tasks	Sort by length	Compare and order by length	Compare and order by height	Sort by weight	Compare by weight	Language of capacity	Language of time	Sequence daily events	Recognition and use of coins	Represent and interpret data

Senior Infants

Senior Infants

Senior Infants Activity Book

Page 20: Noah's ark

Shape and Space: Spatial awareness
Number: Counting

Page 26: The seasons

Number: Comparing and ordering
Number: Counting
Measures: Time

Pages 32-33: The seven dwarfs

Number: Counting
Shape and space: Spatial awareness

Pages 48-49: 1-7

Number: Counting
Algebra: Extending patterns
Shape and space: Spatial awareness

Pages 60-61: In the garden

Number: Counting
Algebra: Extending patterns
Shape and space: Spatial awareness
Shape and space: 2-D shapes
Measures: Length

Pages 76-77: Under the sea

Number: Counting
Number: Analysis of number
Shape and space: Spatial awareness

Page 90: Money

Measures: Money

Page 101: Townscape

Number: Counting
Algebra: Extending patterns
Shape and space: 2-D shapes

Considerable emphasis is placed on the development of problem-solving skills in the *Primary School Curriculum*. Children should work collaboratively, either in pairs or small groups as this assists in the development of communicative skills. The use of manipulatives and concrete materials also assists in this process as the children describe what they observe and what they do with the counters etc.

Page 39: Seven

Begin by exploring the language potential of the story of *The Seven Dwarfs*. Encourage the children to act out the story and make characters using Plasticine.

Using the characters, model a story about the dwarfs e.g. two dwarfs stay in bed while the other five go downstairs for breakfast.

Divide the class into pairs and distribute seven counters to each. Encourage the children to develop and enact stories; one child may tell a story while the other enacts it using the counters. The activity may be recorded pictorially or using Plasticine.

The teacher sits with each group in turn encouraging discussion. When each pair has had the opportunity to tease out their response, there is feedback to the class.

Senior Infants

Strand **Number**

 Objectives

The child should be enabled to:
- count the number of objects in a set (0-20)
- compare equivalent and non-equivalent sets (0-10) by matching
- order sets of objects by number (0-10)
- use the language of ordinal number (first; second; third; last)
- explore the components of number (1-10)
- combine sets of objects, totals to 10
- partition sets of objects (0-10)
- use the symbols + and = to construct word sentences involving addition
- develop an understanding of the conservation of number (0-10)
- read, write and order numerals (0-10)
- identify the empty set and the numeral zero
- estimate the number of objects in a set (2-10)
- solve simple oral and pictorial problems

 Language

count; more than/less than; first/second/third/last; count on; count back; the same as; equals; add; plus; guess; read; write; order

 Materials

Please refer to the materials list on p. 7 for an outline of classroom materials.

You will also need:
- soft toys
- potatoes
- paint
- a fireman's helmet
- brown paper bags
- a football

 Bright ideas (counting and combining)

Posting fun

Seat the children in a circle and stick numbers (1-10) on their backs. One child is designated as post person and carries a post bag filled with old letters and cards. The child walks around the group and beats out the number that appears on each child's back. Each child has to guess how many letters he/she will receive.

Rush to the rescue

Number a series of shoe boxes one to six and place a number of children's toys in each. Divide the class into teams. Each child throws the dice and 'rescues' one toy from that house number. The winning team is the one that 'rescues' most.

Counting conkers

Place up to twenty conkers in a large margarine tub. Encourage the children to scoop up conkers using ladles and yoghurt cartons, to guess how many they have and to verify their guesses. PCM 20 can be used to record this activity.

Fast fingers

Choose a flashcard (1 to 10) and hold it up to the class. Children match it by holding up their fingers as fast as they can. Repeat maintaining a brisk space.

What's in the bag?

Divide the class into pairs and give each pair a number of multilink cubes. One child makes a tower of cubes, places it in a paper bag and removes some of the cubes. The other child then has to establish how many cubes are still in the bag.

Telephone news

To encourage children to learn their telephone numbers, as well as assisting in number recognition, the following rhyme can be used:

'Numbers, numbers everywhere.
Let us play a game.
Please say your telephone number
when I call your name.'

Number pictures

Children can have lots of fun potato printing based on a number story. Printing is done using potato halves and finger painting. For example, a spider might be painted for the number 8 with a potato print body and finger-painted legs.

Dinosaur dinners

Using large paper plates, draw a divider line in the middle of each with a marker. Play the game 'Dinosaur dinners' using dinosaurs or other counters. Children make up their own number stories, e.g. 'I have only 2 dinosaurs for my dinner. I want 3 more. Now I have 5.'

Number ball

Write the numerals zero to five on the panels of a football. The children stand in a circle and pass the ball from one to the other. Initially, each child calls out the numbers nearest their thumbs. As they become accustomed to this activity, they can then begin to combine these numbers. This is quite a dextrous activity and should probably be kept for later in the year.

 **Linkage**

- Colour
- Shape
- Measures
- Data

**Integration**

- Visual arts
- Music
- Physical education
- Geography

Strand **Algebra**

Strand unit

Extending patterns

Page references

Senior Infants Pupil's Activity Book

Extending patterns *pp. 5, 29-30, 97, 101*

 ## Objectives

The child should be enabled to:
- identify, copy and extend patterns in colour, shape, size and numbers (3-4 elements)
- discover different arrays of the same number
- recognise patterns and predict subsequent numbers

 ## Language

pattern; copy; colour; shape; size; how many different patterns?

 ## Materials

Please refer to the materials list on p. 7 for an outline of classroom materials.

You will also need:
- gummed paper shapes
- coloured paper

 ## Bright ideas

Number patterns

Using multilink cubes, encourage the children to learn and explore different ways of making a number.

Circle patterns

In the PE hall or playground, seat the children in a circle and encourage them to experiment with clap and body patterns, for example, stand I stand I sit.

Missing numbers

Attach number cards to a length of clothes line using clothes pegs. Remove some of the numbers and encourage the class to decide which ones are missing.

Shape trail

In Art class, the children cut out large squares, circles, rectangles and triangles. Using two of these shapes, the children make a shape trail pattern along the corridor or in the playground. Possible instructions include asking the children to jump twice on every circle. This activity can be extended using three or four shape types.

Follow the footprints

Using different coloured papers, ask each child to take off a shoe, draw around it and cut out the shoe shape. Using the footprints, the children can then make footprint patterns.

 ## Linkage

- Number
- Shape
- Measures

 ## Integration

- Visual arts
- Music
- Physical education
- Language

Strand units	Page references
Spatial awareness 3-D shapes 2-D shapes	Senior Infants Pupil's Activity Book Spatial awareness *pp. 20, 100* 3-D shapes *pp. 47, 74* 2-D shapes *pp. 6, 13*

 Objectives

The child should be enabled to:
* explore, discuss, develop and use the vocabulary of spatial relations
* sort, describe and name 3-D shapes (cube, cuboid, sphere, cylinder)
* combine 3-D shapes to make other shapes
* solve tasks and problems involving shape
* sort, describe and name 2-D shapes (square, circle, triangle, rectangle)
* combine and divide 2-D shapes to make larger or smaller shapes
* solve problems involving shape and space
* give simple moving and turning directions

 Language

left/right; above/below; near/far; on; beside; in; in front of/behind; cube; cuboid; sphere; cylinder; edge; corner; face; straight; curved; round; flat; square; circle; triangle; rectangle

 Materials

Please refer to the materials list on p. 7 for an outline of classroom materials.

You will also need:
* 2-D linoleum cut-outs
* wooden blocks
* tiles for tessellation
* pencil cases
* hula-hoops

 Bright ideas

Shape faces

Open out a cuboid box and cut it into its component rectangles. Cover each piece with paper and draw a face on each. This activity promotes a discussion of size and shape.

Make more rectangles

Children fold rectangular pieces of paper in half, then in half and then in half again. They then open out the paper and colour in all the new rectangles that they have made.

Sort it out!

Ask the children to bring in different objects from home. In the PE hall, place four hula-hoops in the middle of floor and place one 3-D shape in each. Scatter the objects brought in by the children around the hula-hoops. Play some music and ask the children to locate objects and place them in the appropriate hoop when the music stops.

Marble run

Make a marble run by sticking cuboid bricks to a length of cardboard using Blu-tack. The bricks can be moved around to create different runs.

Shape construction

Cover a variety of objects from the children's environment, such as cereal boxes, kitchen roll and cylindrical crisp containers. Children paint the objects and then explore their constructive qualities and possibilities. It is better not to stick the objects together as this limits their possibilities for construction.

 Linkage

* Comparing and ordering
* Number
* Algebra

Integration

* Physical education
* Visual arts

Senior Infants

Strand unit	Page references
Length	Senior Infants Pupil's Activity Book
	Length *pp. 21-22, 59*

 ## Objectives

The child should be enabled to:

- develop an understanding of the concept of length through exploration, discussion and use of appropriate vocabulary
- compare and order objects according to length or height
- estimate and measure length in non-standard units
- select and use appropriate non-standard units to measure length, width or height

 ## Language

as long as; as wide as; longest/shortest

 ## Materials

Please refer to the materials list on p. 7 for an outline of classroom materials.

You will also need:

- toy cars
- wallpaper samples
- lollipop sticks
- bricks

 ## Bright ideas

Traffic jam

Take a long strip of paper and draw road markings on it, including a set of traffic lights at one end. Children explore the concept of length through play with car counters.

Fill a length

Place marker bricks on two corners of a mat or piece of carpet and ask the children to use enough bricks to fill the distance between the two markers exactly. This activity allows children to explore the concept of measuring length using units.

Footprints on a page

Using different coloured papers, ask each child to take off a shoe, draw around it and cut out the shoe shape. Children then compare their footprints using the language of length.

Decorating time

Using wallpaper samples, the children cover items in the classroom, such as the back of the door and the top of the storage trolley. This activity promotes discussion on the lengths required to cover various objects.

Measuring time

Using lollipop sticks or bricks, the children measure items in the classroom, such as the table or press top.

 ## Linkage

- Number
- Spatial awareness
- Measures

 ## Integration

- Language
- Visual arts

Strand unit	Page reference	Photocopiable master
Weight	Senior Infants Pupil's Activity Book Weight *p. 50*	PCM 13 *p. 72*

Objectives

The child should be enabled to:
- develop an understanding of the concept of weight through exploration, handling of objects and use of appropriate vocabulary
- compare and order objects according to weight
- estimate and weigh in non-standard units
- select and use appropriate non-standard units to weigh objects

Language

heavy/light; heavier/lighter; balance; weigh

Materials

Please refer to the materials list on p. 7 for an outline of classroom materials.

You will also need:
- fruit
- vegetables
- plastic bags
- elastic bands
- a selection of balls

Bright ideas

Weighing bags

Suspend a plastic bag from an elastic band on a hook or stick and place a piece of paper on the wall behind it. The children use the spring balance to compare the weight of a selection of fruit and vegetables by marking the points to which the band stretches on the paper behind.

Buying fruit and vegetables

Visit the local fruit and vegetable shop or supermarket. Weigh the selected items on the shop scales. Back in the classroom, select a piece of fruit and examine how many oranges will balance it.

Lunchbox balance

Children explore the concept of weight by examining how many bricks or beanbags balance full and empty lunchboxes.

Conker balance

Using objects from the classroom, examine how many conkers it takes to balance them. By using PCM 20, this activity can be used to promote estimation and prediction skills.

Compare a ball

Children compare the weights of golf balls, ping pong balls, sponge balls. Their estimates can be verified using the balance.

Linkage

- Number
- Measures

Integration

- Geography
- Language

Senior Infants

Strand unit	Page reference	Photocopiable master
Capacity	Senior Infants Pupil's Activity Book	PCM 14 *p. 73*
	Capacity *p. 46*	

Objectives

The child should be enabled to:
- develop an understanding of the concept of capacity through exploration and the use of appropriate vocabulary
- compare and order containers according to capacity
- estimate and measure capacity in non-standard units
- select and use appropriate non-standard units to measure capacity

Language

holds more/holds less; full/empty; nearly full/nearly empty; too much; too little; too small

Materials

Please refer to the materials list on p. 7 for an outline of classroom materials.

You will also need:
- rice
- pasta
- marbles
- funnels
- sieves
- measuring spoons
- soft toys
- dried peas or beans

Bright ideas

Look and see

Divide an A4 sheet in two. Label one column 'Holds more' and the other 'Holds less'. Children compare the capacity of two different containers by pouring liquid from one into the other and record their findings in the appropriate column on the sheet. To extend this exercise, introduce a third container.

How many

Children estimate and then record how many spoonfuls or eggcups of dried peas or beans it takes to fill another container. Answers may be recorded by drawing and/or writing.

Fill the bucket

Children examine different containers, such as spoons, cups, yoghurt cartons and jugs and discuss how to fill a bucket using them. This activity can be performed in groups or by the entire class, with the children being assigned particular roles.

Take the train

Set out lines of chairs to resemble rows of seats on a train. Designate one child as train driver and another as the ticket seller. The children line up in front of the ticket seller to get their tickets. This activity promotes a discussion of capacity by examining when the train will be full.

Car parks

The children match spaces to cars and compare the numbers of cars in different car parks. A 'spaces empty' board on the car park indicates the number of spaces left. The children change this as each car enters or leaves while discussing the capacity of the car park.

Linkage

- Number
- Time

Integration

- Geography
- Language

Strand unit	Page references	Photocopiable master
Time	Senior Infants Pupil's Activity Book	PCM 15-PCM 17 *pp. 74-76*
	Time *pp. 26, 70-71, 84-85, 87-88*	

Objectives

The child should be enabled to:
- develop an understanding of the concept of time through the use of appropriate vocabulary
- sequence daily and weekly events or stages in a story
- read time in one-hour intervals

Language

yesterday; today; tomorrow; seasons; soon/not yet; birthday; Christmas; St Valentine's Day; St Patrick's Day; Easter; May Day; Hallowe'en

Materials

Please refer to the materials list on p. 7 for an outline of classroom materials.

You will also need:
- clockwork toys
- large sheets of coloured paper

Bright ideas

Beat the timer

Using an egg timer or a clockwork toy, ask the children to estimate and then record how many beads they can thread before the timer/toy stops. This activity promotes estimation and recording skills as well as encouraging development of the concept of time.

Time books

Each child makes his/her own time book from folded sugar paper. The pages are then stamped using a clock stamp. The child fills in each clock stamp and illustrates events that occur at that time.

Weather chart

Cut two circles out of a piece of card. Divide one into quadrants and draw a weather symbol in each. Cut a quadrant out of the second piece of card and place the first piece behind it, attaching them together using a julienne clip. These are simple enough for the children to make, so each child can have his/her own, personalised chart.

Birthday display

Create a wall chart on which each month is marked at the baseline and colour-coded. Give each child a teddy cut-out with space for a label with child's name on front. The children place their cut-outs on the months in which their birthdays fall.

Wall clocks

Make a clock using PCM 15 and a paper fastener. Display the clock on the wall and use it for discussion purposes. The children may like to make and colour their own wall clocks.

Linkage

- Number
- Data

Integration

- Visual arts
- Music
- Physical education

Strand unit	Page references	Photocopiable master
Money	Senior Infants Pupil's Activity Book Money *pp. 90-94*	PCM 18-PCM 19 *pp. 77-78* (PCM 19 to be used from January 2002)

 Objectives

The child should be enabled to:
- recognise coins up to 20p/20 cents and use coins up to 10p/10 cents
- solve practical tasks and problems using money

 Language

cost; price; cheap/expensive; change; too much/too little

 Materials

Please refer to the materials list on p. 7 for an outline of classroom materials.

You will also need:
- newspaper
- real money

 Bright ideas

Under my hand

Cut out a hand shape from old newspaper. Place five pennies/one cent coins in a box and ask the children to take turns hiding some of them under the hand shape. The other children have to decide how many coins are under the hand and how many are left in the box.

Shop fronts

Children make shops using 3-D found shapes, such as cereal boxes. Cover these with white paper and paint them bright colours. Children decorate each box with a different shop front to create a shopping precinct.

Price list

Collect wrappers and juice cartons from the children and stick them on a sheet of A3 paper, writing a price (up to 10p/10 cents) beside each one. Each child brings in ten pennies/one cent coins, five twopences/two cent coins, two fivepences/five cent coins and one tenpence/ten cent coin and practises buying items from the list.

Coin rubbings

Place coins under a thin sheet of paper and use the side of a crayon to take rubbings. This activity assists in coin recognition.

How much does it cost?

A child is given an apple, the price of which is stuck on his/her back. He/she has to question his/her classmates in order to find out how much the apple costs.

 **Linkage**

- Number
- Algebra

 Integration

- Language

Strand unit	Page references	Photocopiable master
Recognising and interpreting data	Senior Infants Pupil's Activity Book Recognising and interpreting data *pp. 7, 31, 40-41, 57, 69, 72, 75, 86, 108-9*	PCM 20 *p.79*

 Objectives

The child should be enabled to:
- sort and classify sets of objects by one and two criteria
- represent and interpret data in two rows or columns using real objects, models and pictures

 Language

more than/less than; more/less; as many as; the same as; enough; as much as; common baseline

 Materials

Please refer to the materials list on p. 7 for an outline of classroom materials.

You will also need:
- hula-hoops
- marbles
- balls
- tin cans
- toy cars
- soft toys

 Bright ideas

Birthday display

Make twelve cardboard balloons by cutting out matching oval shapes and stapling two of these together around the edges. Stuff the balloon with newspaper to create a 3-D effect. Give each child a cut-out to personalise. Write a month on each balloon and affix them to the top of a large sheet of paper. The children position their cut-outs below the appropriate month in horizontal lines.

What do you like to eat?

On a piece of paper, ask the children to draw the faces of three of their friends and three pieces of food they like to eat. They ask each friend in turn what they like to eat and map the response to one of the food items on the page. This activity can be extended by using subjects such as television programmes or sports.

Smelly block graph

Give each child a block and ask the class to brainstorm what smells they like and dislike. Draw a baseline on a sheet of A3 paper and write down a number of the smells discussed. Each child then places his/her block at the smell he/she likes most.

Hula-hoops

Place two hula-hoops on the ground, one labelled 'Big red things' and the other labelled 'Small red things'. Children place objects matching the description in the appropriate hula-hoop.

Bean-bag challenge

Using an egg timer, challenge the children to throw as many bean-bags as they can into a box before the timer empties. Children then count the number of bean-bags in the box and the number that missed. This activity can be used to promote estimation and recording skills.

 **Linkage**

- Colour
- Shape
- Number
- Pattern

 Integration

- Visual arts
- Physical education
- Language

Senior Infants

Write

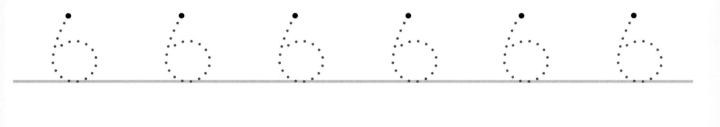

Revisit

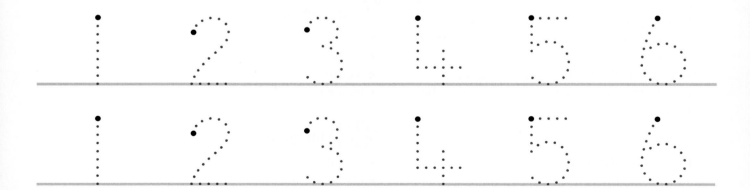

1	2	3	4	5	6	7	8	9	10

Write

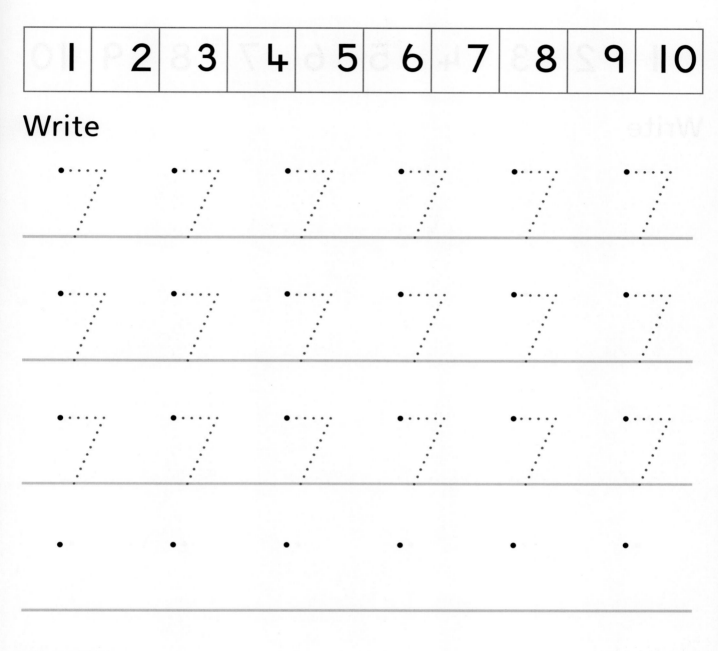

Revisit

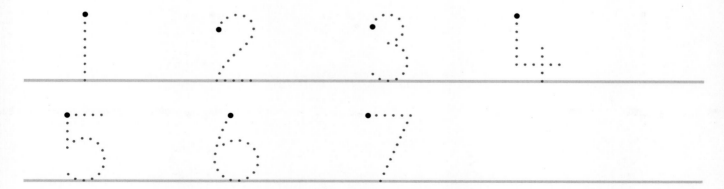

1	2	3	4	5	6	7	8	9	10

Write

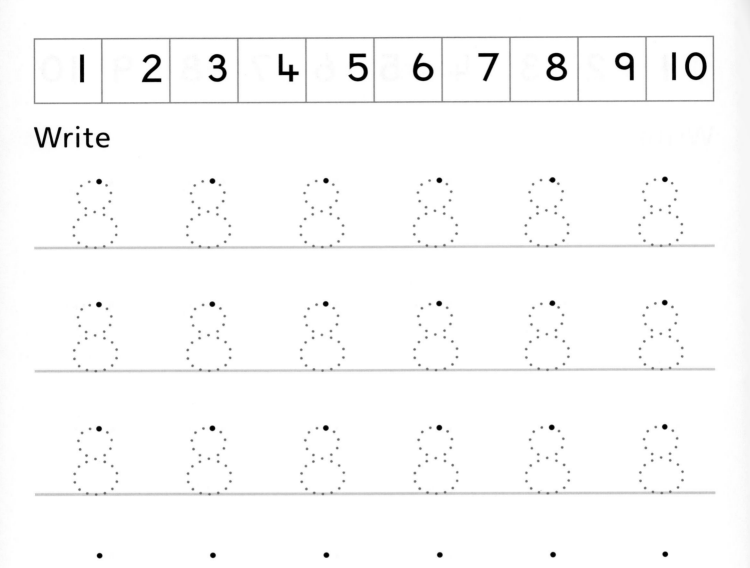

Revisit

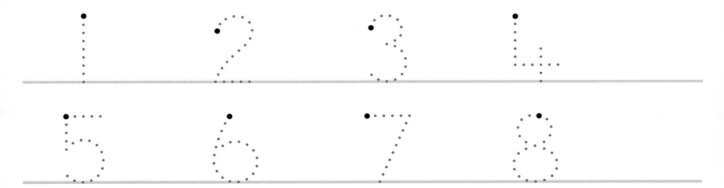

| 1 | 2 | 3 | 4 | 5 | 6 | 7 | 8 | 9 | 10 |

Write

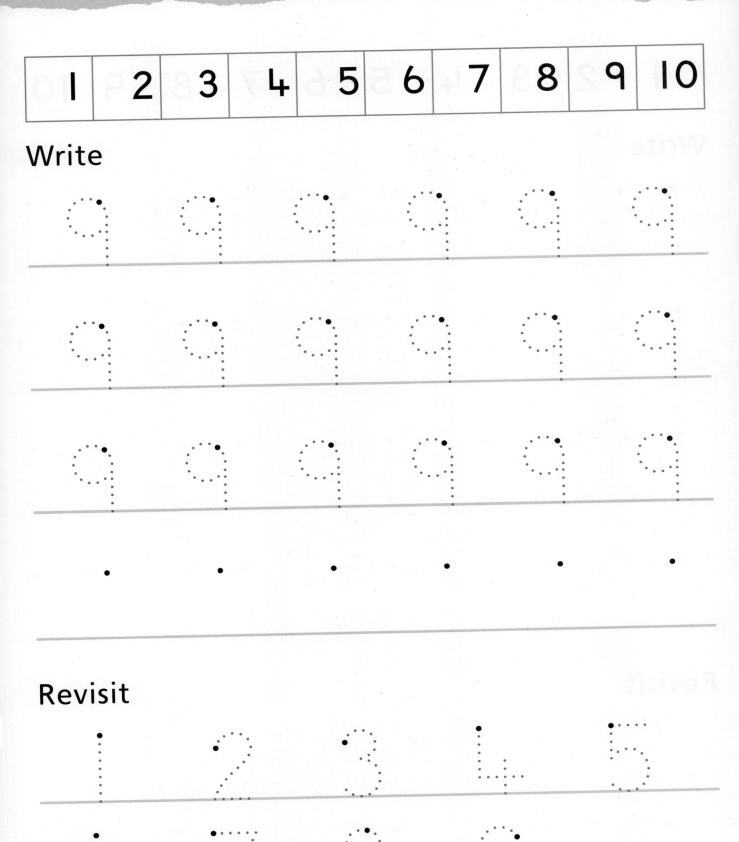

Revisit

| 1 | 2 | 3 | 4 | 5 | 6 | 7 | 8 | 9 | 10 |

Write

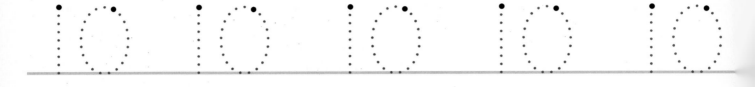

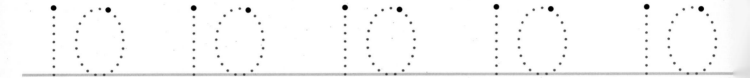

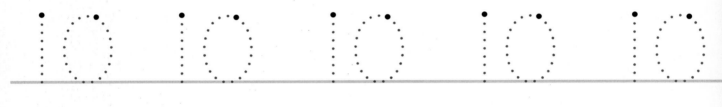

Revisit

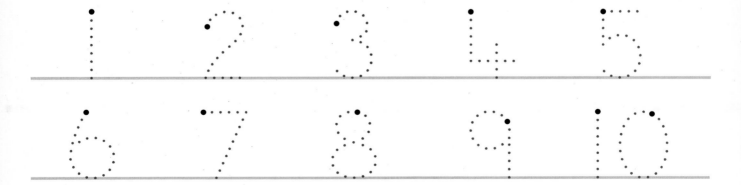

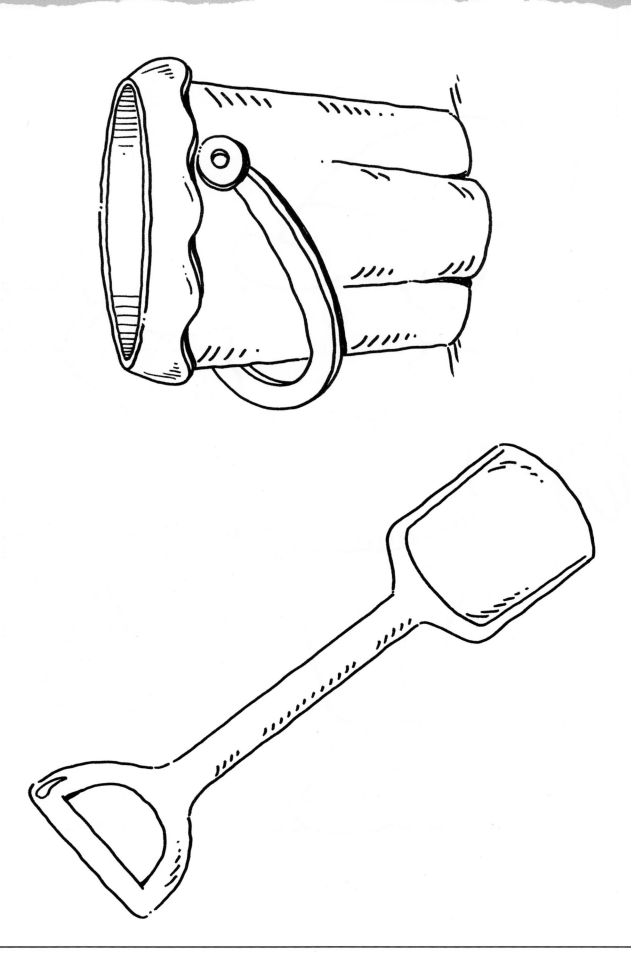

How many?

Draw and colour

Add and colour

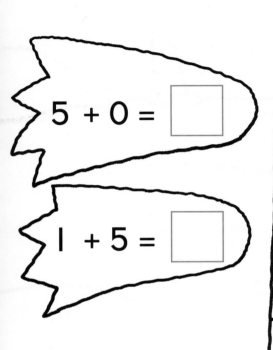

5 + 0 = ☐

1 + 5 = ☐

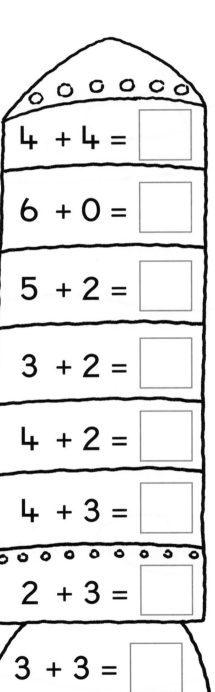

4 + 4 = ☐

6 + 0 = ☐

5 + 2 = ☐

3 + 2 = ☐

4 + 2 = ☐

4 + 3 = ☐

2 + 3 = ☐

3 + 3 = ☐

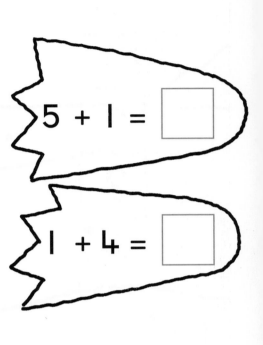

5 + 1 = ☐

1 + 4 = ☐

Add

Colour the heavy things

pots

jugs

mugs

cartons

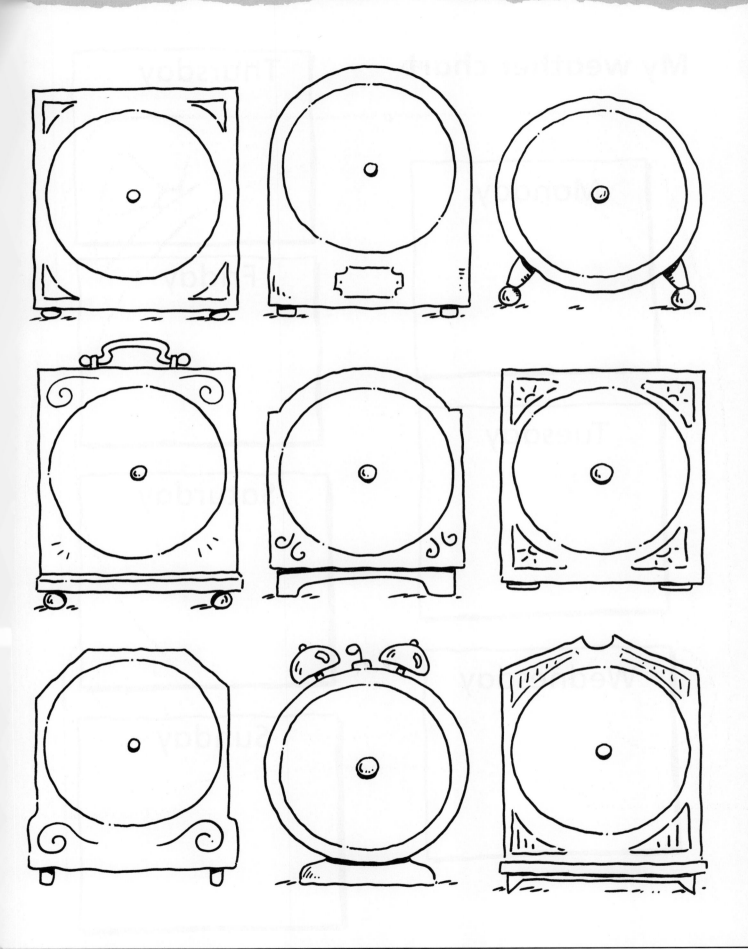

My weather chart

Thursday

Monday

Friday

Tuesday

Saturday

Wednesday

Sunday

Guess

Count

Senior Infants

Ready Steady Maths	Counting	Comparing & ordering			Analysis of number				
Pupil's name	Count objects 1-20	Compare equivalent and non-equivalent sets 0-10	Order sets by number 0-10	Language of ordinal number	Explore components of number 1-10	Combine sets of objects (totals to 10)	Partition sets of objects 0-10	Use the symbol +	Use the symbol =

Analysis of number cont.							Algebra				Spatial awareness	3-D shapes			2-D shapes		
Read numerals 0-10	Write numerals 0-10	Order numerals 0-10	Identify empty set	Identify numeral zero	Estimate sets (2-10)	Solve oral and pictorial problems	Copy and extend colour	Copy and extend shape	Copy and extend size	Copy and extend number	Language of spatial relations	Sort and name 3-D shapes	Combine 3-D shapes	Solve shape tasks	Sort and name 2-D shapes	Combine and divide 2-D shapes	Give moving/turning directions

Senior Infants

	Length				Weight			Capacity				Time			Money			Data
	Compare and order by length	Compare and order by height	Estimate and measure in non-standard units	Selection and use of non-standard units	Compare and order by weight	Estimate and weigh in non-standard units	Selection and use of non-standard units	Language of capacity	Compare and order by capacity	Estimate and measure in non-standard units	Selection and use of non-standard units	Language of time	Sequence events in a story	Read time in hourly intervals	Recognise coins up to 20p/20 cents	Use coins up to 10p/10 cents	Solve tasks using money	Represent and interpret data

Additional activities

Things to do with the Number Line

Make a number line by attaching laminated number cards to a length of wool or thread using large clothes pegs.

- Take a number off the line, ask the class what number is missing and to replace it on the line. As the children become accustomed to the exercise, it can be extended by removing additional numbers.
- Jumble the numbers on the line and ask the class to rearrange them in the correct order.
- Play some music and when it stops, beat out a number. One of the children then goes to the line and removes that number.
- Give each child a sticker with a number on it. Play some music and when it stops, beat out a number. Those children holding that number walk to the number line.
- Draw a number line in the playground. Ask the children to stand on a number and then give them instructions to go forward and back along it.
- Draw a number line in the playground. Using dice, the children count on from the number thrown. The children then move that number of steps on the number line.

Ideas for counting on and counting back

- Children count out a group of toys as they are placed in the magic box. Add more toys and ask the children how many are now in the box. Guesses are verified by counting.
- Using a biscuit tin, drop objects in and encourage the children to count them as you drop them in. The children then turn their backs and continue counting further objects as they are dropped in.
- Place dinosaur, frog and animal counters in a sorting tray. T-Rex comes along and steals some. Children have to find out how many were stolen.
- Children count out a number of counters and hide some of them in a container. They then work out from the remainder how many are in the container and count on to the total.
- The children count three toys on number

mats (carpet samples). Ask them how many will have to be added so that there will be four on each mat.
- The children while sitting down count slowly in unison to ten. They then count back down to zero and jump for blast off.

Things to do with the 'magic box'

Each class should have a number of 'magic boxes' containing specific activities, and which can be circulated on a weekly basis.

- Place various objects including toys, shells and buttons in the box. Children guess what the objects are by feeling them.
- Place pieces of string of different lengths in the box. The children pick one piece each and compare and discuss the lengths of the pieces.
- Place a number of different 3-D shapes in the box. Each child chooses an object without looking and describes its shape to the group. The group has to guess what shape the object is.
- Put five green counters and ten yellow counters in the box. Each child guesses what colour the piece they pull out will be. The children's predictions will become more accurate as number of counters remaining in the box becomes smaller.
- Place a sandwich, a drink carton and an apple in the box. One child looks in the box and gives clues to the class as to the nature of the theme. Through questioning, the class establishes what the theme is.
- Place a number of light and heavy objects in the box. Each child picks one item and predicts whether the next child will select something lighter or heavier.

Ideas for Maths trails

A trail is an activity-based assignment that can take place within the school building, in the school playground or in the locality. Depending on the help available, children can follow the Maths trail in groups or as a whole class with the teacher. Try to get as much help as possible. Emphasise safety rules. Even inside the school grounds, there can be traffic/strangers. Stopping places for observation, discussion and recording need to be clearly identified. Fluorescent arrows to mark the topic might be used.

The trail should include a balance of Maths topics e.g. Shape, Colour and Number. Some tasks should have answers and others should have choice. Include open-ended items to allow for investigation and problem-solving.

Recording can be done either pictorially or orally using a tape recorder for later discussion in class.

Possible topics

- Number: using patio slabs, bricks in wall, window panes etc for estimating and counting tasks
- Number: select items to be counted including trees, posts, doors etc.
- Number: counting problems using number squares and games marked on playground
- Shape: finding 2-D shapes on doors and windows
- Shape: collecting 3-D shapes on the trail and matching them with items in the classroom
- Shape: looking at tessellation in brickwork, paving stones, tiling etc.
- Measures: use of non-standard measures for measuring tasks e.g. paces
- Data: pictorial recording of the information gathered during counting tasks e.g. the number of cars in the car park

Curriculum
planners

Ready Steady Maths

Junior Infants September Starter Curriculum planner

2 *Topic:* Red
Activity: Colour
Strand unit: Classifying

3 *Topic:* Red
Activity: Colour
Strand unit: Classifying

4 *Topic:* Yellow
Activity: Colour
Strand unit: Classifying

5 *Topic:* Yellow
Activity: Colour
Strand unit: Classifying

6 *Topic:* Red
Activity: Draw
Strand unit: Classifying

7 *Topic:* Yellow
Activity: Draw
Strand unit: Classifying

8 *Topic:* Classifying
Activity: Sort by object
Strand unit: Classifying

9 *Topic:* Classify red/yellow
Activity: Colour to sort
Strand unit: Classifying

10 *Topic:* Blue
Activity: Colour
Strand unit: Classifying

11 *Topic:* Blue
Activity: Colour
Strand unit: Classifying

12 *Topic:* Classify red/yellow
Activity: Colour to sort
Strand unit: Classifying

13 *Topic:* Classify blue/yellow
Activity: Colour to sort
Strand unit: Classifying

14 *Topic:* Classify blue/red/yellow
Activity: Colour to sort
Strand unit: Classifying

15 *Topic:* Classify red/yellow
Activity: Colour to sort
Strand unit: Classifying

16 *Topic:* Matching
Activity: Match [identical objects]
Strand unit: Matching

17 *Topic:* Matching
Activity: Match [identical objects]
Strand unit: Matching

18 *Topic:* Yellow
Activity: Colour the circle
Strand unit: Classifying

19 *Topic:* Classify by colour and size
Activity: Colour big/small circles
Strand unit: Classifying

20 *Topic:* Matching
Activity: Match [related objects]
Strand unit: Matching

21 *Topic:* Matching
Activity: Match [related objects]
Strand unit: Matching

22 *Topic:* Matching
Activity: Match & draw [related objects]
Strand unit: Matching

23 *Topic:* Teddy bears' picnic
Activity: Oral language page incorporating a colour activity
Strand unit: Comparing

24 *Topic:* In the adventure playground
Activity: Oral language page incorporating a colour activity
Strand unit: Comparing

key

Early mathematical activities

90 Junior Infants Activity Book Curriculum planner

1
Topic: Classify red/yellow
Activity: Colour to sort
Strand unit: Classifying

2
Topic: Classify blue/yellow
Activity: Colour to sort
Strand unit: Classifying

3
Topic: Big
Activity: Colour the big objects
Strand unit: Comparing

4
Topic: Classify yellow/red/blue
Activity: Colour to sort
Strand unit: Classifying

5
Topic: Matching
Activity: Match [identical objects]
Strand unit: Matching

6
Topic: Matching
Activity: Match [related objects]
Strand unit: Matching

7
Topic: Jack and the beanstalk
Activity: Oral language
Strand unit: Comparing

8
Topic: Bigger
Activity: Colour the bigger objects
Strand unit: Comparing

9
Topic: Smaller
Activity: Ring the smaller objects
Strand unit: Comparing

10
Topic: Size
Activity: Oral language
Strand unit: Ordering

11
Topic: Matching
Activity: Match & draw [related objects]
Strand unit: Matching

12
Topic: Matching
Activity: Match & draw [related objects]
Strand unit: Matching

13
Topic: Triangle
Activity: Ring the triangles
Strand unit: 2-D shapes

14
Topic: Triangles big/small
Activity: Colour to sort
Strand unit: 2-D shapes

15
Topic: Triangle; circle
Activity: Colour to sort
Strand unit: 2-D shapes

16
Topic: 1
Activity: Write
Strand unit: Analysis of number

17
Topic: 1
Activity: Draw
Strand unit: Analysis of number

18
Topic: 1
Activity: Colour
Strand unit: Analysis of number

19
Topic: 1
Activity: Ring sets of 1
Strand unit: Analysis of number

20
Topic: Long
Activity: Colour the long objects
Strand unit: Length

21
Topic: Short
Activity: Ring the short objects
Strand unit: Length

22
Topic: Long
Activity: Draw longer objects
Strand unit: Length

23
Topic: Long; short
Activity: Draw shorter objects
Strand unit: Length

24
Topic: 2
Activity: Write
Strand unit: Analysis of number

25
Topic: 2
Activity: Write
Strand unit: Analysis of number

26
Topic: 2
Activity: Write
Strand unit: Analysis of number

27
Topic: 2
Activity: Draw
Strand unit: Analysis of number

28
Topic: 2
Activity: Draw
Strand unit: Analysis of number

29
Topic: 2
Activity: Ring sets of 2
Strand unit: Analysis of number

30
Topic: How many? (1-2)
Activity: Write
Strand unit: Counting

31
Topic: The pond
Activity: Oral language
Strand unit: Spatial awareness

32
Topic: Square
Activity: Ring the squares
Strand unit: 2-D shapes

33
Topic: Triangle; circle; square
Activity: Colour to sort
Strand unit: 2-D shapes

34
Topic: 3
Activity: Write
Strand unit: Analysis of number

35
Topic: 3
Activity: Write
Strand unit: Analysis of number

36
Topic: 3
Activity: Write
Strand unit: Analysis of number

37
Topic: 3
Activity: Draw
Strand unit: Analysis of number

38
Topic: 3
Activity: Draw
Strand unit: Analysis of number

39
Topic: 3
Activity: Ring sets of 3
Strand unit: Analysis of number

40
Topic: How many? (1-3)
Activity: Write
Strand unit: Counting

41
Topic: Shapes
Activity: Oral language
Strand unit: 3-D shapes

42
Topic: Pattern
Activity: Colour to extend
Strand unit: Extending patterns

43
Topic: Pattern
Activity: Colour to extend
Strand unit: Extending patterns

44
Topic: Pattern
Activity: Colour to extend
Strand unit: Extending patterns

45
Topic: Heavy; light
Activity: Oral language
Strand unit: Weight

46
Topic: 4
Activity: Write
Strand unit: Analysis of number

47
Topic: 4
Activity: Write
Strand unit: Analysis of number

48
Topic: 4
Activity: Write
Strand unit: Analysis of number

49
Topic: 4
Activity: Ring sets of 4
Strand unit: Analysis of number

50
Topic: 4
Activity: Make 4
Strand unit: Analysis of number

51 *Topic:* 1–4
Activity: Colour
Strand unit: Counting

52 *Topic:* Time
Activity: Oral language
Strand unit: Time

53 *Topic:* How many? (1–4)
Activity: Write
Strand unit: Counting

54 *Topic:* 1–4
Activity: Match
Strand unit: Analysis of number

55 *Topic:* First; last
Activity: Colour
Strand unit: Comparing & ordering

56 *Topic:* Full; empty
Activity: Ring
Strand unit: Capacity

57 *Topic:* First; last
Activity: Colour
Strand unit: Comparing & ordering

58 *Topic:* 5
Activity: Write
Strand unit: Analysis of number

59 *Topic:* 5
Activity: Write
Strand unit: Analysis of number

60 *Topic:* 5
Activity: Write
Strand unit: Analysis of number

61 *Topic:* 5
Activity: Draw
Strand unit: Analysis of number

62 *Topic:* 5
Activity: Ring sets of 5
Strand unit: Analysis of number

63 *Topic:* 5
Activity: Make 5
Strand unit: Analysis of number

64 *Topic:* 1–5
Activity: Colour
Strand unit: Counting

65 *Topic:* 1–5
Activity: Colour
Strand unit: Analysis of number

66 *Topic:* Narrow; wide
Activity: Oral language
Strand unit: Length

67 *Topic:* Money
Activity: Colour to sort
Strand unit: Money

68 *Topic:* Rectangle
Activity: Ring & draw
Strand unit: 2-D shapes

69 *Topic:* Triangle; circle; square; rectangle
Activity: Colour to sort
Strand unit: 2-D shapes

70 *Topic:* How many?
Activity: Prediction & recording
Strand unit: Recognising & interpreting data

71 *Topic:* How many? (1–5)
Activity: Write
Strand unit: Counting

72 *Topic:* 1–5
Activity: Match
Strand unit: Analysis of number

73 *Topic:* Empty set
Activity: Oral language
Strand unit: Analysis of number

74 *Topic:* Zero
Activity: Ring & write
Strand unit: Analysis of number

75 *Topic:* How many?
Activity: Make & record
Strand unit: Analysis of number

76 *Topic:* How tall?
Activity: Prediction & recording
Strand unit: Recognising & interpeting data

77 *Topic:* Shape
Activity: Extend & count
Strand unit: 2-D shapes

78 *Topic:* Money
Activity: Colour to sort
Strand unit: Money

79 *Topic:* Data
Activity: Oral language
Strand unit: Recognising & interpreting data

80 *Topic:* Data
Activity: Oral language
Strand unit: Recognising & interpreting data

81 *Topic:* How many?
Activity: Combining
Strand unit: Analysis of number

82 *Topic:* How many?
Activity: Combining
Strand unit: Analysis of number

83 *Topic:* Shape
Activity: Make
Strand unit: 3-D shapes

84 *Topic:* How many? (1–5)
Activity: Write
Strand unit: Counting

85 *Topic:* Townscape
Activity: Oral language
Strand unit: Extending patterns

86 *Topic:* How many?
Activity: Write & draw
Strand unit: 2-D shapes

87 *Topic:* Pattern
Activity: Copy & draw
Strand unit: Extending patterns

88 *Topic:* How many?
Activity: Prediction & recording
Strand unit: Recognising & interpeting data

89 *Topic:* 1–5
Activity: Write the missing numbers
Strand unit: Comparing & ordering

90 *Topic:* Countdown
Activity: Oral language
Strand unit: Analysis of number

91 *Topic:* 1–5
Activity: Write
Strand unit: Counting

92 *Topic:* 1–5
Activity: Write the missing numbers
Strand unit: Comparing & ordering

93 *Topic:* 1–5
Activity: Match
Strand unit: Analysis of number

94 *Topic:* Bug trail
Activity: Oral language
Strand unit: Recognising & interpreting data

key

Early mathematical activities

Number

Algebra

Shape and space

 Measures

 Data

Senior Infants Activity Book Curriculum planner

1 Topic: Matching
Activity: Match [related objects]
Strand unit: Comparing & ordering

2 Topic: 1–5
Activity: Colour
Strand unit: Counting

3 Topic: 0–5
Activity: Write
Strand unit: Counting

4 Topic: 0–5
Activity: Match
Strand unit: Analysis of number

5 Topic: Pattern
Activity: Copy & extend
Strand unit: Extending patterns

6 Topic: Shape
Activity: Colour to sort
Strand unit: 2-D shapes

7 Topic: How many?
Activity: Ring to sort
Strand unit: Recognising & interpreting data

8 Topic: How many?
Activity: Write
Strand unit: Counting

9 Topic: How many?
Activity: Combining
Strand unit: Analysis of number

10 Topic: Is the same as
Activity: Draw
Strand unit: Analysis of number

11 Topic: Is the same as
Activity: Write
Strand unit: Analysis of number

12 Topic: Counting on
Activity: Write
Strand unit: Analysis of number

13 Topic: Shape
Activity: Colour
Strand unit: 2-D shapes

14 Topic: 6
Activity: Write
Strand unit: Analysis of number

15 Topic: 6
Activity: Write
Strand unit: Analysis of number

16 Topic: 6
Activity: Write
Strand unit: Analysis of number

17 Topic: 6
Activity: Draw
Strand unit: Analysis of number

18 Topic: 6
Activity: Ring sets of 6
Strand unit: Analysis of number

19 Topic: 6
Activity: Make 6
Strand unit: Analysis of number

20 Topic: Noah's ark
Activity: Oral language
Strand unit: Spatial awareness

21 Topic: Longest
Activity: Colour the longest objects
Strand unit: Length

22 Topic: Shortest
Activity: Colour the shortest objects
Strand unit: Length

23 Topic: Is the same as
Activity: Draw & write
Strand unit: Analysis of number

24 Topic: How many?
Activity: Write
Strand unit: Analysis of number

25 Topic: How many?
Activity: Write
Strand unit: Analysis of number

26 Topic: The seasons
Activity: Oral language
Strand unit: Time

27 Topic: First; last
Activity: Colour
Strand unit: Comparing & ordering

28 Topic: First; second; third
Activity: Colour
Strand unit: Comparing & ordering

29 Topic: Pattern
Activity: Draw & colour
Strand unit: Extending patterns

30 Topic: Pattern
Activity: Draw
Strand unit: Extending patterns

31 Topic: Data
Activity: Draw
Strand unit: Recognising & interpreting data

32 Topic: The seven dwarfs
Activity: Oral language
Strand unit: Analysis of number

33 Topic: The seven dwarfs cont.
Activity: Oral language
Strand unit: Analysis of number

34 Topic: 7
Activity: Write
Strand unit: Analysis of number

35 Topic: 7
Activity: Write
Strand unit: Analysis of number

36 Topic: 7
Activity: Draw
Strand unit: Analysis of number

37 Topic: 7
Activity: Ring sets of 7
Strand unit: Analysis of number

38 Topic: 7
Activity: Make 7
Strand unit: Analysis of number

39 Topic: 7
Activity: Combining
Strand unit: Analysis of number

40 Topic: Data
Activity: Draw & colour
Strand unit: Recognising & interpeting data

41 Topic: Data
Activity: Draw & colour
Strand unit: Recognising & interpreting data

42 Topic: Add
Activity: Write
Strand unit: Analysis of number

43 Topic: Add
Activity: Write
Strand unit: Analysis of number

44 Topic: Add
Activity: Write
Strand unit: Analysis of number

45 Topic: Add
Activity: Write
Strand unit: Analysis of number

46 Topic: Full; empty
Activity: Colour
Strand unit: Capacity

47 Topic: Shape
Activity: How many?
Strand unit: 3-D shapes

48 Topic: 1–7
Activity: Write
Strand unit: Counting

49 Topic: 1–7 cont.
Activity: Write
Strand unit: Counting

50 Topic: Heavy; light
Activity: Colour
Strand unit: Weight

51 Topic: 8
Activity: Write
Strand unit: Analysis of number

52 Topic: 8
Activity: Write
Strand unit: Analysis of number

53 Topic: 8
Activity: Draw
Strand unit: Analysis of number

54 Topic: 8
Activity: Ring sets of 8
Strand unit: Analysis of number

55 Topic: 8
Activity: Make 8
Strand unit: Analysis of number

56 Topic: 8
Activity: Combining
Strand unit: Analysis of number

57 Topic: 8
Activity: How tall?
Strand unit: Prediction & recording
Strand unit: Recognising & interpreting data

58 Topic: 8
Activity: Counting on
Strand unit: Write
Strand unit: Analysis of number

59 Topic: Tallest; shortest
Activity: Colour
Strand unit: Length

60 Topic: In the garden
Activity: Oral language
Strand unit: Analysis of number

61 Topic: In the garden cont.
Activity: Oral language
Strand unit: Analysis of number

62 Topic: 9
Activity: Write
Strand unit: Analysis of number

63 Topic: 9
Activity: Write
Strand unit: Analysis of number

64 Topic: 9
Activity: Draw
Strand unit: Analysis of number

65 Topic: 9
Activity: Ring sets of 9
Strand unit: Analysis of number

66 Topic: 9
Activity: Make 9
Strand unit: Analysis of number

67 Topic: 9
Activity: Combining
Strand unit: Analysis of number

68 Topic: Counting back
Activity: Colour
Strand unit: Analysis of number

69 Topic: Data
Activity: Draw & colour
Strand unit: Recognising & interpreting data

70 Topic: Time
Activity: Oral language
Strand unit: Time

71 Topic: Time
Activity: Write
Strand unit: Time

72 Topic: Data
Activity: Draw & colour
Strand unit: Recognising & interpreting data

73 Topic: More; less
Activity: Ring
Strand unit: Comparing & ordering

74 Topic: Shape
Activity: Colour to sort
Strand unit: 3-D shapes

75 Topic: Data
Activity: Draw & colour
Strand unit: Recognising & interpreting data

76 Topic: Under the sea
Activity: Oral language
Strand unit: Analysis of number

77 Topic: Under the sea cont.
Activity: Oral language
Strand unit: Analysis of number

78 Topic: 10
Activity: Write
Strand unit: Analysis of number

79 Topic: 10
Activity: Write
Strand unit: Analysis of number

80 Topic: 10
Activity: Draw
Strand unit: Analysis of number

81 Topic: 10
Activity: Ring sets of 10
Strand unit: Analysis of number

82 Topic: 10
Activity: Make 10
Strand unit: Analysis of number

83 Topic: 10
Activity: Combining
Strand unit: Analysis of number

84 Topic: Days of the week
Activity: Write
Strand unit: Time

85 Topic: Days of the week cont.
Activity: Write
Strand unit: Time

86 Topic: Data
Activity: Draw
Strand unit: Recognising & interpreting data

87 Topic: Time
Activity: Write
Strand unit: Time

88 Topic: Time
Activity: Write
Strand unit: Time

89 Topic: Counting
Activity: Write
Strand unit: Counting

90 Topic: Money
Activity: Oral language
Strand unit: Money

91 Topic: Money
Activity: Colour
Strand unit: Money

92 Topic: Money
Activity: How many?
Strand unit: Money

93 Topic: Money
Activity: Match
Strand unit: Money

94 Topic: Money
Activity: Colour
Strand unit: Money

95 Topic: Add
Activity: Write
Strand unit: Analysis of number

96 Topic: Add
Activity: Write
Strand unit: Analysis of number

97 Topic: Missing numbers
Activity: Write
Strand unit: Extending patterns

98 Topic: Add
Activity: Write
Strand unit: Analysis of number

99 Topic: Add
Activity: Write & colour
Strand unit: Analysis of number

100 Topic: Left; right
Activity: Draw
Strand unit: Spatial awareness

101 *Topic:* Townscape
Activity: Oral language
Strand unit: Extending patterns

102 *Topic:* Zero
Activity: Write
Strand unit: Analysis of number

103 *Topic:* Zero
Activity: Write
Strand unit: Analysis of number

104 *Topic:* 10
Activity: Make 10
Strand unit: Analysis of number

105 *Topic:* 10
Activity: Make 10
Strand unit: Analysis of number

106 *Topic:* How many?
Activity: Write
Strand unit: Analysis of number

107 *Topic:* How many?
Activity: Write
Strand unit: Analysis of number

108 *Topic:* Guess & count
Activity: Write
Strand unit: Recognising & interpreting data

109 *Topic:* Guess & count
Activity: Write
Strand unit: Recognising & interpreting data

110 *Topic:* Add
Activity: Write & colour
Strand unit: Analysis of number

key

 Number

 Algebra

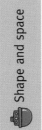 Shape and space

 Measures

 Data

Notes

Notes

Ready Steady Maths